777 Poems

M. Ray Allen

Foreword by: Charles Billingsley, recording artist and teaching pastor at Thomas road baptist church, Lynchburg, VA

Mountain Empire Publications

777 Poems
All Rights Reserved.
Copyright © 2024 M. Ray Allen
v2.0

This is a work of poeticized fiction. The opinions expressed in this manuscript are solely the opinions of the author and do not represent the opinions or thoughts of the publisher. The author has represented and warranted full ownership and/or legal right to publish all the materials in this book.

This book may not be reproduced, transmitted, or stored in whole or in part by any means, including graphic, electronic, or mechanical without the express written consent of the publisher except in the case of brief quotations embodied in critical articles and reviews.

Mountain Empire Publications

ISBN: 978-0-9970341-9-6

Cover Design by Chloe Vess © 2024 Mountain Empire Publications. All rights reserved - used with permission.

PRINTED IN THE UNITED STATES OF AMERICA

Acknowledgements

The author expresses grateful acknowledgment to the following for their assistance in proofreading the manuscript, assistance in navigating the computer, and editing suggestions: Landon Ray Allen, Anmarie R. Herald, Layla DePriest, and Heidi Mullins.

Contents

Foreword	i
777 Poem Defined	iii
Dedication	v
777 Poem #1	1
777 Poem #2	3
777 Poem #3	5
777 Poem #4	7
777 Poem #5	9
777 Poem #6	11
777 Poem #7	13
Study Guide	15
Seven Questions for #1	16
Seven Questions for #2	17
Seven Questions for #3	18
Seven Questions for #4	19
Seven Questions for #5	20
Seven Questions for #6	21
Seven Questions for #7	22
Answer Section for #1	23
Answer Section for #2	25
Answer Section for #3	27
Answer Section for #4	29
Answer Section for #5	31
Answer Section for #6	33
Answer Section for #7	35
The Poet	37

Foreword

Ray Allen is a good man. He's had such a rich history of artistry and in helping other Virginian musical artists through the years, that he is a deeply loved individual across this country.

But he is also a poet. This book of poetry is unique. I've never seen poetry like this, in that every single line contains only one syllable words. That takes a lot of work and creativity. For that reason alone, I can appreciate Ray's efforts here. But Ray also loves Jesus. And through this poetry, he wants to see people come to faith in Christ and grow in Him.

I think you will enjoy this book and learn from it, as well.

Charles Billingsley

Charles Billingsley, a nationally prominent recording artist, songwriter, and pastor who was born in Clovis, New Mexico in 1970 and grew up in Alabama, has headlined more than 3,000 concerts across the country, including ones at such venues as the Kennedy Center and Carnegie Hall. Seven of his recordings have become No. 1 hits on Inspirational radio, and he has 24 recordings to his credit as a solo artist.

As a teenager in Alabama, Charles performed as a vocalist with a teenage gospel music group, and after graduating from Samford University in Birmingham, he became the lead vocalist with New Song, a Grammy-nominated gospel music group, from 1994-1997. He has continued to perform as a solo artist after leaving the group.

As a member of The Virginia Opry, the Commonwealth of Virginia's official Opry since 2020, Charles has performed as the headliner on The Virginia Opry in Clifton Forge, Virginia and at the Natural Bridge Historic Hotel and Conference Center's Washington Hall in Natural Bridge, Virginia.

At the time of publication, Charles is serving as a teaching pastor at Thomas Road Baptist Church in Lynchburg, Virginia, and he continues to tour and share the good news about his Lord and Savior, Jesus Christ.

777 Poem Defined

A 777 Poem is comprised of seven stanzas, each stanza containing seven lines, and each of the seven lines consisting of seven monosyllabic words with the first word of each of the seven stanzas beginning with the word, "Christ."

Dedication

I dedicate the *777 Poems* to Milford Hall, Sr., my mother's father who was a primitive Baptist preacher in McDowell, Kentucky, for 40 years and the author of *Two Worlds* and *What Think Ye of Christ?*, the last book that he wrote. As a senior at McDowell High School in 1959, I typed his manuscript for *What Think Ye of Christ?*, using my Underwood typewriter as he read his handwritten manuscript to me, often rephrasing his words, requiring me to make changes while he kept reminding me of my need to develop patience.

777 Poem

Christ walked on sea near small boat
While men on board gazed at Him.
One walked from boat to greet Christ,
But his faith gave way to waves
Till Christ reached and took his hand.
Dubbed the "Rock" by Christ, the man
Came to be head of Christ's church.

Christ wrote in dirt of the yard
While men stood with stones in hands.
Told the man who had no sin
To cast the first stone at her,
The lass they had come to kill.
Once they dropped their stones and left,
Christ bade, "Go and sin no more!"

Christ rubbed mud on the man's eyes
So he could see light of day,
Then used spit to heal one more.
All who saw Christ heal the blind
Spread the news from town to town
The King of the Jews had come
To share God's Light with all men.

Christ knelt on stone near high cliff
To test His strength as a man.
No food for days, He felt pain
As Old Scratch came to test Him.
Clad in faith, Christ passed each test
Old Scratch laid out to lead Christ
To break His bond with the Lord.

Christ broke bread with twelve He loved;
Passed the cup that knights would seek
As their quest to prove their worth.
Christ knew which one would leave Him
As they shared their one last meal,
For Christ knew His time had come
To bear the sins of the world.

Christ wept as His hour drew near,
Wept while those who loved Him slept,
Wept as He prayed to please God.
Not one prayed with Christ that night
As sleep proved to be too strong
For them to keep watch with Christ
Who knew His last day had come.

Christ rose from the dead one day,
The third as He said He would.
Showed nail holes in hands to one
Who lacked faith in his own eyes
Till Christ led that man to see
That his faith was flawed by doubt
That Christ would rise from the dead.

777 Poem

Christ led men to hear Him speak
There on the mount where He preached
To men He bade to show love
For God who sent Him to share
The good news that Christ is God,
The Word Who formed all of Earth
Where He had now come to dwell.

Christ showed that He is God's Son,
That all of His words and deeds
Came from God who gave Him Light
As Son of Man here on Earth
Where He healed a man so sick
That for years he could not walk
Till Christ told him to get up.

Christ said that He would lay down
His life one day for His sheep,
Said some not yet His would hear
His words and come to join Him
As the Son of God made Flesh
To show them Light void of dark
In which they would find no Light.

Christ said that He would ask God
To send Help to dwell in each
Of loved ones He would soon leave
That each could do the good works
That He had led them to do.
Then when Christ left those He loved,
God sent Help to guide them all.

Christ told Jews to keep His word,
Those who chose to walk with Him,
Told them that they would know truth,
And that truth would make them free,
Told them all who sin are slaves,
But that the Son will free them
If they hear and keep His word.

Christ told Jews who heard His news
But chose not to heed His word
That they live to serve Old Scratch,
Told those who wished to kill Him
That they would not dwell with God
But serve dark to end in dark
Where all weep and gnash their teeth.

Christ told all with ears to hear
That they would not taste of death
If they chose to keep His word,
Told them they did not know God
For God had sent Him to them
That they may live in God's house
Should they choose Him to find Light.

777 Poem

Christ took two fish and five loaves,
Thanked God for the loaves and fish
The lad had brought there with him,
Bade the crowd to sit on grass
So all could be fed by those
Christ chose to spread the good news
That food for all could be had.

Christ turned and picked up some cords
To serve as His whip that day
He drove out those who sold stock
In God's house here on the Earth.
Bade them not to spoil God's house,
To keep it clean for God's work--
Not for their own greed and gain.

Christ is the Word who made Earth
And all that was made with it.
As flesh, the Word dealt with pain,
Dealt with the will of the flesh
That the Word had not dealt with
In time till His birth on Earth
Where He came to share God's Light.

Christ turned to wine what filled pots
That had been filled from the well.
Hailed by the guests at the feast
As best wine saved last to serve,
The wine Christ gave those who wed
Was fruit of Christ's first good work
To show He and God are One.

Christ wept as He neared the cave
Where the dead man had been placed.
There Christ bade the dead man rise,
And out from the tomb he came,
Limbs still wrapped in the death cloth
His loved ones had clad him with
Four days prior to what Christ did.

Christ said He came not to judge
But to save the world from sin,
Said His word would judge the world
On the last day here on Earth,
Said He came to give men Light
And that His words came from God
Who sent Him here as His Son.

Christ rose in sky to leave Earth
While all who watched Him stood by,
For He told them He would leave
To set up a place for them
In God's house where they would dwell
In bliss with Him void of pain,
The good news they spread that day.

777 Poem

Christ said that those who make peace
Shall be called the Sons of God;
Said the pure in heart are blessed,
That His are salt of the earth
And His the Light of the world
That is to be shown to all,
Not for them to hide from men.

Christ slept on a boat with friends,
The ones He chose as His flock.
But a great storm stirred the sea
And sent waves to swamp the boat.
Christ's men woke Him due to fear;
He did chide them for flawed faith,
Then calmed both the sea and wind.

Christ bade men He chose to lead,
To shake off dust from their feet
If those in homes did not heed
The good news of words they brought
To help those lost see the Light
That Christ had taught each to share
By word of mouth to save souls.

Christ bade men to love their wives
The way Christ loves His own church,
Said man and wife are one flesh,
That God made the wife for birth
And man to sow the good seed
As he clings to one he wed,
Save she strays to lie with men.

Christ bid those who heard Him speak
To love God with all their strength,
Heart, soul, and mind as their link
From Earth to dwell with the Lord
Where there is no pain or death,
Just true bliss and praise for God
Where there are no woes to have.

Christ warned that false Christs would come
To claim they were sent from God,
But all His would know their ruse
If clad in the words Christ taught
That not one of His could fall
For a fake Christ from the dark
Sent by Old Scratch to fool them.

Christ cast out those deemed not clean,
Ones that dwelt in boys and girls
To make them ill with no cure
Till Christ bid the not clean leave
And taught those He led to act
Out what He had done to heal
Those who had the dark in them.

777 Poem

Christ said a house will not stand
If kept by more than just one
For God dwells as King of kings
Void of dark and full of Light
That shines bright for all to see
That in the House of the Lord
No dark can dwell as in hell.

Christ came through a field of grain
Where He paused to pluck for food
On the day God made for rest.
Jews who set out to blame Him
For His act that broke their law
Were shocked when Christ said to them,
"Son of Man is this day's Lord."

Christ sat in a boat and taught
As the crowd sat by the sea
While He told of those who sow
Seeds that birds fly down to eat,
Seeds on rocks with soil too thin
To help roots take hold to live,
And seeds that sprout in good earth.

Christ told that three men were hired
To pick grapes for pay one day,
One at the start of day's work,
One who was hired late to pick,
And one hired at the last hour.
Then all three were paid the same,
But some deemed their pay not fair.

Christ told the Jews God sent Him
To share the good news on Earth
That He had come as the Light
To lead men out of the dark
Where they love the lie, not truth.
Christ told those who buy the lie
They will not live in God's house.

Christ felt one not seen touch Him
On His robe and felt the cure
Take place by faith that mere touch
Could heal should one's faith be strong.
Christ turned and asked who it was
For He knew her faith was true,
The kind He had come to give.

Christ said that men do not live
By just bread but by God's word,
Said words that He shares with men
Come not from Him but from God
Who sent Him to share the Light
So men who dwell in the dark
Can be saved from all their sins.

777 Poem

Christ said to those that He led
His food is to do God's will
And to do the work of God,
Told them to lift up their eyes
And look at the fields so white
They were ripe to reap for Him,
And some would sow and some reap.

Christ told the scribe that one God
Is the Lord of all on Earth,
And one should love his one Lord
With all his heart, soul, and mind
And strength to serve God each day.
Christ then told him that he should
Love those next door as one's self.

Christ healed the man near the pool,
The lame one who could not rise
To reach the pool to be healed.
Christ saved the man from his sins,
Then bade him rise and go home.
Those who saw the lame man walk
Knew that he was healed by God.

Christ knew His own sheep by name,
Told them He would lead His flock,
That each of His sheep would come
To the sound of His own voice,
And all who see Him see God
For the Son of Man came here
To lay down His life for them.

Christ bled from nails the man drove
Through both of His hands and feet
On Christ's cross near the two thieves.
Christ chose to save one who asked
That Christ save him as he bled.
The one who mocked Christ that day
Died on the cross lost in sin.

Christ on cross cried out in pain
From nails in both hands and feet
While He shed His blood for sins
Of the world He came to save.
The crown of thorns that He wore
Was placed on His head in jest
By those who came to mock Him.

Christ bled from His crown of thorns
Where print read "King of the Jews"
As those who drove nails stood by
And cast lots for all His clothes
Till earth quaked and sky grew dark.
Then they knew what they had done
As Christ breathed out His last breath.

777 Poem

Christ sent word to John locked up
To tell him the blind can see,
The lame can walk and deaf hear,
And that those not clean are healed.
Told them to tell that those dead
Have been raised up for more life
And that the poor hear God's word.

Christ bade the men that He chose
To let their good works be seen,
Called them the salt of the earth
And pure of heart who were blessed
As the true light of the world.
Christ then laid out His true plan
That they should bring in His sheep.

Christ made mute speak and deaf hear
And lame to get up and walk,
Used His spit to heal the blind.
Those who saw, said Christ did well
On all who came to be healed.
Yet there were those who would kill
Christ for his works as God's Son.

Christ told the rich man who asked
What he should do to please God
That he should sell all he had,
Then give his gain to the poor
So he could dwell in God's house
And walk with Christ here on Earth.
Sad, the young man went his way.

Christ spoke of the place called hell
Where those who dwell in dark go
To gnash their teeth while they weep.
Then Christ told of God's free gift
That all can claim if they wish
To live in Light void of dark
That sin has brought to the Earth

Christ asked what a man would gain
If he were to gain the world
But lose his soul as he did.
Christ bade each one who sought Him
To pick up his cross and come
To walk with the Son of Man
That he may live in God's house.

Christ, the Word Who was with God,
Came to the Earth He had made
While He dwelt with God as One
To make all seen and not seen,
Then to live as Son of Man,
Born to serve as God made flesh
To guide all men to the Light.

Study Guide

On the following pages, one question pertains to each stanza of each of the seven poems; each poem composed of seven monosyllabic lines provides the reader with an opportunity to enter into a discussion concerning the content of each poem.

777 Poem on Pages 1 and 2

Stanza 1: Who was the "Rock?"

Stanza 2: Why were the men gathered to stone the woman to death?

Stanza 3: What two methods did Christ use to heal the two blind men?

Stanza 4: Who came to test Christ?

Stanza 5: What name has been given to the cup that Christ drank from at the Last Supper?

Stanza 6: Where did Christ spend His last night before being crucified?

Stanza 7: Who was the one who lacked faith?

777 Poem on Pages 3 and 4

Stanza 1: What does Christ reveal to His followers about the foundation of the Earth?

Stanza 2: What did Christ reveal about the Word becoming flesh and dwelling here on Earth?

Stanza 3: What metaphor does Christ use to name His followers?

Stanza 4: What does Christ mean by promising to send Help?

Stanza 5: What future event is Christ referring to?

Stanza 6: What did Christ tell the Jews would happen to them if they rejected His word?

Stanza 7: What did Christ reveal as His mission to all with ears?

777 Poem on Pages 5 and 6

Stanza 1: How could two fish and five loaves of bread feed a large crowd?

Stanza 2: Why did Christ drive people out of God's house?

Stanza 3: What verse in *The Bible* reveals that the Word was with God from the beginning and the Word was God?

Stanza 4: What was Christ's first miracle?

Stanza 5: Who was the dead man, Christ brought back to life?

Stanza 6: What mission here on Earth does Christ reveal?

Stanza: 7: What was Christ's purpose for ascending into the sky?

777 Poem on Pages 7 and 8

Stanza 1: As revealed by Christ, who will become the Sons of God?

Stanza 2: Why did Christ's followers awaken Him?

Stanza 3: Why did Christ tell His disciples to shake the dust from their feet?

Stanza 4: What did Christ reveal the purpose of a man's wife is?

Stanza 5: What link to God did Christ share?

Stanza 6: What did Christ reveal to His disciples would save them from a future false Christ?

Stanza 7: What is the term used today for removing unclean spirits from those possessed?

777 Poem on Pages 9 and 10

Stanza 1: Who did Christ identify as being void of dark and full of Light?

Stanza 2: What law of the Jews was broken?

Stanza 3: What did Christ mean when He spoke about the seed?

Stanza 4: In the parable that Christ shares, what point does He make about becoming born again?

Stanza 5: What does the dark represent?

Stanza 6: Why did the woman receive healing without asking Christ to heal her?

Stanza 7: Who did Christ say provided Him with the messages He delivered to men?

777 Poem on Pages 11 and 12

Stanza 1: What did Christ identify as His food?

Stanza 2: Who does Christ identify as worthy of being loved with one's heart, soul, and mind?

Stanza 3: Where did Christ tell the lame man to go after He healed him?

Stanza 4: What did Christ reveal as His reason for coming to Earth?

Stanza 5: Which one of the two thieves did Christ save?

Stanza 6: For whom did Christ shed His blood on the cross?

Stanza 7: What physical conditions surrounding the cross changed before Christ breathed His last breath?

777 Poem Pages 13 and 14

Stanza 1: What were the miracles that Christ revealed to John via a messenger?

Stanza 2: Who did Christ call " ... the salt of the earth?"

Stanza 3: Why did some Jews seek to kill Christ?

Stanza 4: Why did the rich man decide not to follow Christ?

Stanza 5: Where did Christ reveal that those who dwell in dark go?

Stanza 6: What do you think that Christ meant when He said that anyone who seeks to follow Him should pick up his cross and come walk with Him?

Stanza 7: Who formed the Earth?

Answer Section:

Please note that some answers will vary because some of the questions are posed to elicit what the reader thinks in order to stimulate discussion.

Pages 1 and 2, Answers

Stanza 1: Christ posed the question, "Who am I?" The Apostle Peter answered,
"You are God." Christ said that God has revealed the truth to you and upon that rock of truth He would build His Church.

Reference: *Matthew* 14: 22-33

Stanza 2: The woman had been caught committing adultery.

Reference: *John* 7:53--8:11

Stanza 3: Christ rubbed mud on one blind man's eyes to heal him, and He used His spit to restore another blind man's sight.

Reference: *Mark* 8 and *John* 9: 1-38

Stanza 4: Old Scratch, which is another name for Satan, came to tempt Christ to disobey God, the Father.

Reference: *Matthew* 4: 1-11

Stanza 5: The name given to the cup that Christ drank from during the Last Supper came to be known as the Holy Grail or the Holy Chalice.

Reference: *Luke* 22: 11-20

Stanza 6: Christ spent His last night before being crucified in the Garden of Gethsemane.

Reference: *Matthew* 26: 36-56

Stanza 7: Saint Thomas did not believe that Christ had risen from the dead until Christ instructed him to touch Him and see the nail holes in His hands.

Reference: *John*: 20: 24-27

Pages 3 and 4, Answers

Stanza 1: Christ revealed that He formed the Earth before He emptied Himself of His powers as the Word to become flesh here on Earth.

Reference: *Matthew* 5: 1-12

Stanza 2: Christ revealed that He is God's Son here on Earth.

Reference: *Luke* 5: 18-25

Stanza 3: He uses the word, "sheep," to identify his followers.

Reference: *John* 10: 11-18

Stanza 4: Christ uses the word, "Help," to identify the Holy Spirit that God would send to indwell Christians at Pentecost and serve to guide born again Christians for future generations.

References: *John* 14: 16, 2 *Corinthians* 1:22, 5: 5, and *Ephesians* 1: 13-14

Stanza 5: The judgement is what Christ is referring to when He tells the Jews that they will be saved providing they hear His message and keep His word.

Reference: *Romans* 6: 15-19

Stanza 6: Christ told the Jews that they would not dwell with God.

References: *John* 12: 48 and *Matthew* 25: 30

Stanza 7: Christ revealed that those who chose to keep His word that they would live in God's House where they would dwell in Light rather than dark.

Reference: *Matthew* 16:28

Pages 5 and 6

Stanza 1: The two fish and five loaves of bread fed the large crowd because Christ performed a miracle to feed the crowd.

Reference: *Luke* 9: 13-17

Stanza 2: Christ drove out those selling stock because they were desecrating the House of God.

Reference: *Mark* 21: 12-13

Stanza 3: John 1:1 reveals that the Word was with God from the beginning and that the Word was God.

Reference: *John* 1:14

Stanza 4: The first miracle Christ performed was at a wedding where He turned water into wine.

Reference: *John* 2: 11

Stanza 5: Lazarus was the name of the dead man that Christ brought back to life from the grave.

Reference: *John* 11: 38-45

Stanza 6: Christ reveals that His mission on Earth is to provide a plan of salvation to save the world from sin.

Reference: *John* 5: 26-29

Stanza 7: Christ promised those who watched Him ascend into the sky that He did so to prepare a place for them in His Father's house where there are many mansions.

References: *Acts* 1: 9-11 and *John* 14: 3

Pages 7 and 8

Stanza 1: Christ revealed that those who make peace shall be called " ... the Sons of God."

Reference: *Matthew* 5: 9

Stanza 2: Christ's friends, who were his followers, awakened Him because they were afraid of the storm.

Reference: *Matthew* 8: 23-27

Stanza 3: Christ instructed His followers to shake the dust off their feet if those they witnessed to did not believe the good news they shared with them.

Reference: *Matthew* 10: 14

Stanza 4: Christ led the Apostle Paul to reveal that men should love their wives the way Christ loves His church and that wives should revere their husbands.

Reference: *Ephesians* 5: 25-33

Stanza 5: Christ revealed that strong faith and devotion to loving God is the link they need to establish in order to dwell with God after they die.

Reference: *Luke* 10: 27

Stanza 6: Christ revealed to His followers that they could clad themselves in the words He taught in order to avoid being fooled by false Christs in the future.

Reference: *Matthew* 24: 4-14

Stanza 7: The term for expelling an unclean spirit from one possessed is "exorcism," the act of removing an unclean spirt by an exorcist.

References: *Mark* 3: 15, *Mark* 6: 7

Pages 9 and 10

Stanza 1: Christ identified God the Father as being full of Light and void of dark.

Reference: *Matthew* 12: 25

Stanza 2: Christ was accused of breaking the Jewish Sabbath day.

Reference: *Matthew* 12: 1

Stanza 3: Christ taught by using parables, and the seeds, the message He delivered from God the Father, could only be fruitful by being received by those who believe as identified in the parable as the " ... good earth."

Reference: *Matthew* 13: 1-23

Stanza 4: Christ reveals that sinners may become born again at different stages of life, but that all who receive salvation receive the same heavenly reward, eternal life in God's house.

Reference: *Matthew* 20: 1-16

Stanza 5: The dark represents the sinful state of existence mankind is experiencing by not accepting the good news of redemption that Christ brought with Him to lead sinners out of the dark.

Reference: *Matthew* 15: 24

Stanza 6: Because of her strong faith in Christ, the woman who had been hemorrhaging without being cured for 12 years received healing by touching Christ's garment.

References: *Luke* 8: 43-48 and *Matthew* 9: 20-22

Stanza 7: Christ credits God the Father for providing Him with the messages that He delivered to men.

Reference: *Matthew* 4: 4

Pages 11 and 12

Stanza 1: Christ identified His food as doing the will of God.

Reference: *John* 4: 35-38

Stanza 2: Christ reveals that God the Father is worthy of being loved with one's heart, soul, and mind.

Reference: *Matthew* 22: 37-40

Stanza 3: After Christ healed the lame man by the healing pool, He told him to pick up his bed and walk.

References: *John* 5: 1-15, *John* 5: 7

Stanza 4: Christ revealed to His followers that His purpose on Earth was to die for them, thus completing God's plan of salvation.

Reference: *John* 10: 13-15

Stanza 5: Christ saved the thief on the cross who asked for Christ to save him but did not save the thief who mocked Him.

Reference: *Luke* 23: 42-43

Stanza 6: Christ shed His blood on the cross for the sins of the world in order to complete God's plan of salvation for sinners.

Reference: *Matthew* 27: 29

Stanza 7: The Earth quaked and darkness prevailed prior to Christ's death on the cross.

Reference: *Matthew* 27: 35

Pages 13 and 14

Stanza 1: Christ revealed that He was performing miracles: healing the blind, the lame, the deaf, those possessed by unclean spirits, and raising of the dead.

Reference: *Matthew* 11: 4-5

Stanza 2: Christ chose His disciples to let their good works be seen and to become known as "the salt of the earth."

Reference: *Matthew* 5: 13-20

Stanza 3: Some sought to kill Christ because He claimed to be equal to God.

Reference: *Matthew* 11: 5

Stanza 4: The rich man decided not to follow Christ because he valued his riches more than he valued Christ's message of salvation.

References: *Matthew* 19: 16-30, *Mark* 10: 17-31, and *Luke* 18: 18-30

Stanza 5: Christ reveals that those who embrace the dark instead of the Light will go to hell where they will gnash their teeth and weep.

References: *Luke* 16: 19-31, *Romans* 6: 23, and *Ephesians* 2: 8

Stanza 6: The act of picking up the cross to follow Christ represents the commitment a Christian makes to living to please God by following the teaching of Christ.

Reference: *Mark* 8: 3-38

Stanza 7: The Word formed the Earth before the Word emptied Himself of His heavenly powers to become God in the flesh, Jesus Christ.

Reference: *John* 1: 14

The Poet

The *777 Poems* is M. Ray Allen's fifth collection of poems following *The Roads I Travel*, Nightshade Press, Troy, Maine (1990); *Between the Thorns: Windcarver Songs of Appalachia*, ROAD Publishers, Fairfax Station, Virginia (1991); *Beyond Star Bottom and Other Poems*, Mountain Empire Publications, Clifton Forge, Virginia (2000); and *An Appalachian Poet in San Francisco*, Mountain Empire Publications, Clifton Forge, Virginia (2013). Allen made his debut as a poet as a featured reader at the opening ceremony for the Douglass House Center in Long Beach, California in 1968, where Budd Schulberg served as the keynote speaker.

The University of Tennessee Press published *Encyclopedia of Appalachia* in 2006, featuring Allen as follows: "M. Ray Allen, a poet and Appalachian activist from Clifton Forge, Virginia, is a native of Martin, Kentucky, whose writing and teaching career led him to help Appalachian youth through literacy and the performing arts. A high school teacher since 1963, Allen is best known for his work as founding director of Appalfolks of America, a nonprofit corporation that promotes drug-free living through its writing and performance programs. Appalfolks owns and operates the historic Stonewall Theatre in Clifton Forge as a performance center for Appalachian youth. Allen's poems are widely published in literary arts magazines across the United States and in four book-length volumes."

The Morehead State University Alumni Hall of Fame inducted Allen as its 80th member in 1991, citing his literary achievements, community service work with Appalfolks, and his career as an educator as its criteria for the honor. Allen has won more than 40 poetry awards, 16 of which were for poems that won first-place-cash-prizes for contests such as

"An Appalachian Poet in San Francisco" that in 2013, won The Beat of Our Own Drum Poetry Contest sponsored by the Green River Writers of Louisville, Kentucky.

Additionally, he has read his poems at the Berkeley Poets' Co-Op, UCLA, Virginia Tech, Radford University, Berea College, Roanoke's Center in the Square, Southern Seminary, Appalshop, Jenny Wiley State Park Amphitheatre, Jenny Wiley State Park's May Lodge, Douthat State Park Amphitheatre, Mountain Gateway Community College, Clifton Forge Public Library, Historic Stonewall Theatre, Paramount's Kings Dominion in Doswell, Virginia, and at bookstores in Virginia and Kentucky.

Allen served as the sports editor of *The Tattler*, McDowell High School's newspaper, and he earned varsity letters in baseball at MHS in 1958 and 1959. At Morehead State University, he earned three varsity letters in baseball, served as sports reporter and feature story writer for *The Trail Blazer*, MSU's student newspaper; and played centerfield for the City of Morehead's Kentucky State Semi-Pro Tournament championship team, batting .333 for the tournament during which he made a game-saving defensive play and hit a three-run home run. As a baseball player, he played on eight championship baseball teams, and as an honor student, he was elected as president of his senior class at both MHS and MSU.

After graduating from MSU with his A.B. degree with a double major in English and physical education in 1963, Allen was hired as the varsity basketball and baseball coach at Lewis County High School in Vanceburg, Kentucky, where he taught journalism, creative writing, physical education, and health from 1963 till 1965, the year he earned his M.A. degree in secondary education from MSU. Despite his team's 0-13 start during his first year of coaching varsity basketball in 1963-1964, his LCHS's Lions won the first 63rd District

Tournament championship in the consolidated school's history by defeating three teams that had defeated his Lions during the 13-game losing streak.

After signing a contract to teach English and serve as varsity baseball coach at Fraser High School near Detroit in 1965, Allen continued writing poetry, and a number of his poems such as "The Poison Apple" and "South of Toledo" were inspired by the grist he gathered in Michigan where he coached his team to the best record and finish in the school's history by defeating Lakeview High School, the 22-0 district champions, by a 2-0 score in the Bi-County Tournament and by going on to finish as the runner-up team after losing the championship game 2-1 to South Lake High School.

Allen accepted an English teaching position at Marina High School in Huntington Beach, California, in 1967, and he was soon hired to coach freshmen basketball for Lute Olson, the varsity coach of the Vikings who went on to coach in college and lead the University of Arizona to win the NCAA basketball championship in 1997. While being employed to teach English and physical education at MHS, Allen began attending poetry and screenwriting workshops in the area, and he served as varsity baseball coach of the MHS's Vikings for four years, leading his team during his third year of coaching to qualify for the CIF Playoffs for the first time in the school's history. His Vikings repeated the feat by competing in the CIF Playoffs again the next year.

Often spending his summer vacations traveling, Allen spent one summer in Berkeley and often visited with Linda Gregg and Jack Gilbert in San Francisco. Before moving to California, he had befriended the two poets at a writers' workshop conducted at Alice Lloyd College by Albert Stewart, Allen's creative writing professor and mentor at MSU. It was the same summer that he became a friend of Joe DiMaggio and discovered that they had a mutual friend in Steve Hamilton, an All-American basketball player at MSU who went on to pitch for the New York Yankees and play in the NBA. Hamilton happened to be pitching for the San Francisco Giants that summer. Nearly 20 years later, Hamilton attended Allen's induction into the MSU Alumni Hall of Fame where Allen recited "DiMaggio Smiles," the poem he wrote, one published in Westwind: *UCLA's Quarterly of the Arts*.

During the summer of 1970, Allen traveled abroad to Japan, Hong Kong, India, Egypt, Tanzania, Kenya, Ethiopia, Greece, and England, and while driving across the United States in 1971, he met his wife to be, Cherie Suzanne Davis, a resident of Alleghany County, Virginia. Davis, a graduate of Alleghany County High School, won the Miss Virginia title in 1968, while she was a student at Shenandoah University in Winchester, Virginia, and she won her talent division as a vocalist, finishing as a Top Ten Finalist in the Miss America Pageant.

The couple were married in Long Beach, California in 1973, during the time Cherie was performing in *Gigi*, the Lerner and Lowe production that was being staged at the Dorothy Chandler Pavilion in Los Angeles before the musical made its way to Broadway. Prior to their marriage, Cherie had performed with two Los Angeles Civic Light Opera productions and toured the U.S. and Canada with productions of *The Sound of Music* and *Fiddler on the Roof*.

Before Ray was hired to coach the varsity basketball team at Alleghany County High School in Low Moor, Virginia in 1978, where Cherie had painted the Colt, the school's mascot which was on display in the gymnasium where Ray would coach his team, he had completed his course work for his M.F.A. degree in theater arts at UCLA where he majored in writing for television and motion pictures, and his first poem to be published, one he wrote about Uncle Sam stripping Mohammed Ali of his heavyweight boxing title, had been published in *Black Times*, a literary arts magazine based in Palo Alto, California.

While serving as varsity basketball and varsity golf coach at ACHS, Ray sponsored the Fellowship of Christian Athletes and Appalfolks in Action, a club that helped students get in touch with their Appalachian heritage by attending Appalachian youth conferences at Radford University and the University of West Virginia.

Prior to his return to Appalachia in 1978, Ray's YPF physical fitness team had won the Southern California championship by defeating Crawford High School of San Diego, and he had coached three freshmen basketball teams to championships, one finishing with a 20-0 record. After returning to Appalachia, Ray coached the only varsity basketball championship team in ACHS's 20-year history when his Colts won the Blue Ridge District Tournament held at Washington & Lee University in 1981. By then, he had finished writing *Bloody Harlan*, an original screenplay, to complete the requirements for receiving his M.F.A. degree from UCLA.

As a freelance journalist, Ray has hundreds of credits for articles published in newspapers and magazines, mostly publications such as *Golf Review*, *Day Tripper*, *The Daily Review*, and *The Virginian Review*, a daily newspaper established in Covington, Virginia in 1914. After serving as a stringer for The Virginian Review, he was hired as the editor in 2022, after the newspaper had become a tri-weekly publication. His column, "Domain of No Spin," ran in *The Virginian Review* during the 14 months he served as the editor.

Prior to receiving the Historic Stonewall Theatre (currently operating as The Historic Masonic Theatre), Appalfolks teamed with Total Action Against Poverty (TAP) to form the first adult literacy program in the Alleghany Highlands, and the Alleghany County Board of Supervisors designated both organizations as official literacy agents.

By 1991, Appalfolks was conducting a creative writing outreach at the Augusta Correctional Center in Craigsville, Virginia, where Ray served as the outreach coordinator and poetry workshop leader. Before ending the outreach, Ray received an honorary award for his volunteerism from the prison's warden. In December of that year through Ray's efforts, Irwin R. Cohen, R-C Theatre's owner, donated the Historic Stonewall Theatre to Appalfolks.

For the next 12 years, Ray served as the theatre manager and spearheaded the restoration of the twin-cinema to its original purpose, a performing arts theatre (circa 1905), before persuading the board of directors to donate the theatre to the Town of Clifton Forge in 2003. By that time, Appalfolks had made more than $200,000 worth of restoration improvements, and Ray had written two two-act dramas that were staged in the theatre: *A Musical Tribute to the Railroad* and *The Life and Times of Mad Ann Bailey*, a play that received a favorable review in the *News-Gazette* in Lexington.

In 1996, Appalfolks formed Special Theatrical Artists Review and Showcase (STARS), a troupe of ten performers who had physical disabilities or faced intellectual challenges. *STARS* has grown to 30 members who perform three variety shows per year. In 2006, Appalfolks' documentary film titled STARS won a Bronze Telly, and recently, *STARS* is featured in the December/January 2023-2024 issue of *Moose*. Ray spearheaded the forming of STARS, named the troupe, and continues to write press releases for STARS and work hand-in-glove with Paula Crance and Sonya Romonella, the co-directors.

On October 17, 1992, The Virginia Opry, an Appalfolks musical outreach, made its debut with a troupe of 10 performers. Ray currently serves as the director of The Virginia Opry which was honored by the Commonwealth of Virginia General Assembly in 2017, via "House Resolution 397" for producing country music shows in the Alleghany Highlands for 25 consecutive years. The Virginia Opry became the Commonwealth of Virginia's official Opry on March 31, 2020, when Governor Ralph S. Northam signed "Senate Bill 283" which was filed by Senator R. Creigh Deeds. Since then, The Virginia Opry has established a new attendance record and a new box office record at The Historic Masonic Theatre and has performed shows in Richmond, Charlottesville, Roanoke, Natural Bridge, Lexington, and Covington.

After Ray and Cherie purchased the Buckhorne Country Store and Campground in 2000, Ray retired in 2004. Having held varsity coaching positions in four states during his 41-year-career as an educator, Ray taught the following subjects at one time or another: English, journalism, reading, creative writing, mythology, screenplay writing, drama, photography, physical education, health, and hunter's safety. He also coached winning teams in baseball, basketball, golf, cross country, and YPF physical fitness

Ray and Cherie have lived on their Rainbow Ridge Ranch in Alleghany County since 1979, and they are the parents of four grown children: Landon Ray Allen, a graduate of VMI who served as an F-18 Hornet pilot and fought against the Taliban in Afghanistan as a Captain in the U.S. Marine Corps and who is now employed by Southwest Airlines as a pilot; Jana Allen Bahrns, a graduate of Liberty University and the William Esper Studio in Manhattan who as a vocalist and actress has landed roles on such TV shows as *The Office*, *George and Tammy*, *Manhunt Unabomber*, and *The Righteous Gemstones* in addition to performing in many movies, including the leading-lady role in *Remember Yesterday: A Wilmington Love Story*; Amber Suzanne Dean, a graduate of the Staunton School of Cosmetology who now operates the Amber Suzanne Salon at the Buckhorne; and Anmarie Herald, a graduate of Mountain View Community College and a former airline attendant for Piedmont Airlines who has served as the manager of the Buckhorne.

Ray may be the only poet to win a poetry contest and a trophy for fighting in a karate tournament during the same year. He has studied the martial arts under six black belts, including Mike Stone, winner of 96 consecutive black belt matches. He is a member of the Honorable Order of Kentucky Colonels, and he has served as the Grand Marshall of the Clifton Forge Christmas Parade, received the Elks Distinguished Citizenship Award from the Benevolent and Protective Order of Elks, been honored by the Clifton Forge Public Library via a display of his achievements during National Poetry Month in 2023, and received an award by Sankar Enterprises for his role in restoring the Historic Stonewall Theatre.

As a songwriter, Ray has written or co-written five songs that have been professionally recorded, including "Home Sweet Home, Virginia," the song he co-wrote with the late Bob Campbell, one of six vocalists to tour as one of The Statler Brothers. The song has been released as the people's choice for the state song of Virginia following their entry finishing in the Final 20 out of 339 entries into the Virginia State Songwriting Contest held by the Commonwealth of Virginia in 1998. "Home Sweet Home, Virginia," finished first in two of the contest's five criteria categories, second in one, fourth in another, and eighth in the fifth category that the judges were instructed to consider before making their decisions concerning their song selections. Although no song was chosen as the new state song due to irregularities in the contest judging process, "Home Sweet Home, Virginia" has become The Virginia Opry's official theme song.

Milton Keynes UK
Ingram Content Group UK Ltd.
UKHW031034020824
446373UK00001B/74

9 780997 034196